NEW COLLECTION

Adult Coloring Book
Stress Relieving Mandala Designs

**PAT
WOODS**

Adult Coloring Book

Stress Relieving Mandala Designs

Pat Woods

Thanks for purchasing Pat Woods's Adult Coloring Book: Stress Relieving

Animal Designs.

We recommend you also to get her other books:

Adult Coloring Book: Amazing Designs

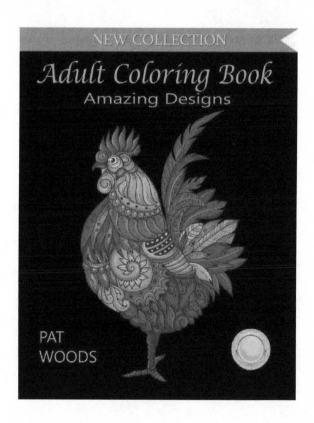

You can purchase it on this Link:

https://www.amazon.com/dp/1717999263

Adult Coloring Book: Stress Relieving Animal and Unicorn

Designs

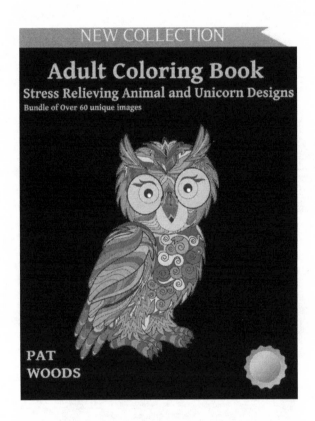

You can purchase it on this Link:

https://www.amazon.com/dp/1718087640

Adult Coloring Book: Stress Relieving Unicorn Designs

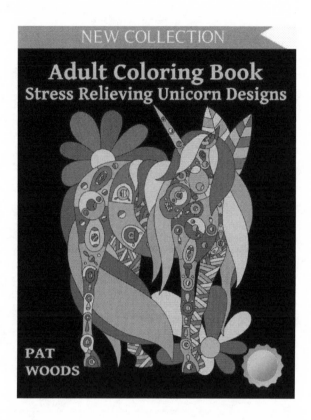

You can purchase it on this Link:

https://www.amazon.com/dp/1718025513

Adult Coloring Help Relieve Stress and Anxiety

here has been a huge wave about adult coloring books. Coloring books are no nger just for children. It is now advocated by therapists, psychologists, healers nd alternative medicine practitioners as an effective form of fighting off stress. It even advocated as an alternative to meditation.

he American Art Therapy Association has even done a study on "Art Therapy" hich includes adult coloring books. It is incredible how powerful an adult oloring book can be.

can reduce stress, bring self-awareness, increase self-esteem, develop social ills, improve your sense of reality, reduce anxiety and panic. Not to mention the reative benefits of it, as a means of self-expression, a fantastic creative outlet.

also brings about mindfulness. There is a lot of tranquility in coloring an image.

Ve recommend you do not use crayons but coloring pencils for more precision nd relaxation.

Enjoy this coloring book and take your time! 😊

Thank You!

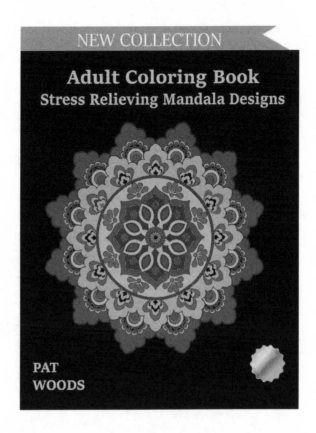

Thank you for purchasing my book.

I hope that the Adult Coloring Book made you feel relaxed and calm and that you enjoyed the journey of your inner exploration.

Practice coloring into your daily life for a Peaceful, Positive Mind.

Thanks for purchasing Pat Woods's Adult Coloring Book: Stress Relieving Animal Designs.

We recommend you also to get her other books:

Adult Coloring Book: Amazing Designs

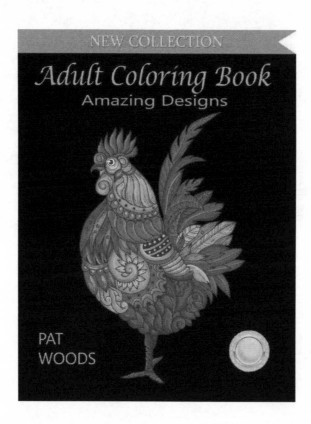

You can purchase it on this Link:

https://www.amazon.com/dp/1717999263

Adult Coloring Book: Stress Relieving Animal and Unicorn

Designs

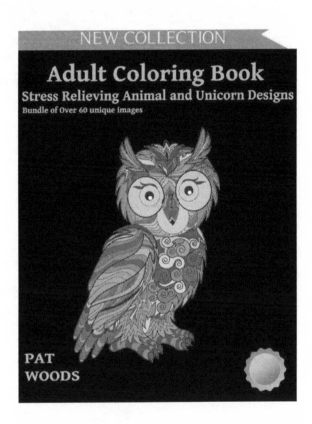

You can purchase it on this Link:

https://www.amazon.com/dp/1718087640

Adult Coloring Book: Stress Relieving Unicorn Designs

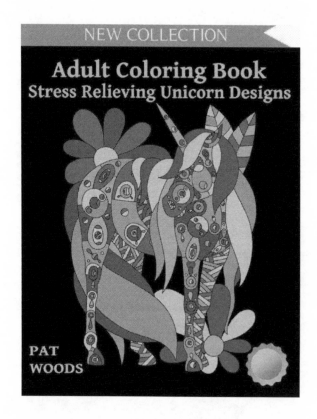

You can purchase it on this Link:

https://www.amazon.com/dp/1718025513

Made in the USA
Lexington, KY
06 December 2018